Introduction

Many people consider themselves to be either hand or machine embroiderers while others combine the two successfully. With a mixture of the two techniques we have a vast and exciting palette at our disposal. Most typically this is worked by machine stitching into a background with hand stitching used to further embellish the piece.

In this booklet we will look at TWO quite distinct approaches to combining hand and machine stitching in dynamic ways that can offer vigorous and dimensional surfaces as well as subtle and fragile effects. Both methods are capable of being worked in limitless ways to produce practical or wall hung textiles. They are also relatively unexplored and very versatile.

Following our philosophy of giving pointers and guidelines we hope to encourage you to consider our suggestions in the first instance before developing them in your own style.
This is just the tip of the iceberg and we hope there are enough tantalising samples to encourage you to try for yourself with many more avenues to follow.

Inside Front Cover:
A simple machined grid of straight stitches darned with a range of knitting tapes, fabric strips and embroidery silks in matt, shiny and metallic textures.

Right:
Machined straight stitch lines and circular shapes decorated with straight and buttonhole stitches plus the addition of tiny crystal beads.

Useful Pointers

The most useful advice we can give to anyone anticipating working with their machine is to get to know it and be comfortable handling the basic functions. The techniques we are developing are relatively simple and require the minimum of adjustments.

• Large top stitch needles either 100 or 110 (not less than 90) will help.

• Initially select a good-tempered thread and one that you know works well for you and your machine.

• Wooden circular frames with bound inner frames make for ease of working.

• Although many people work with a foot attachment we both advocate the use of a darning foot to stabilise the fabric and avoid thread breakage. There are excellent darning feet that allow maximum visibility available for most machines.

• If you are new to free motion stitching then follow the makers instructions for setting up the machine and first experiment with spirals or other rhythmic patterns on a firm fabric held taut in frame.

• We both keep ongoing notebooks with samples and suggest that all samples could be kept in a small notebook with simple notes on tensions etc as you go.

• If you really do not need any more samples then they would make delightful cards etc (see 'Giving Pleasure' - book 8).

Armed with these simple guidelines we are ready to proceed.

Hand Stitching onto Machine Stitched Networks - by Jan

In this section of the book constructive starting points are made whereby machine stitch provides a base structure and a foil for hand stitches to feature prominently. It is an unusual approach with exciting possibilities.

The advent and subsequent development of water soluble fabric has enabled the adventurous machine embroiderer to make a wonderful array of stitched artefacts. It is now possible to create new fabrics exploiting textural surfaces, lacy or gossamer meshes. Although hand stitch is the main feature, fabric snippets, beads and other assorted materials may be successfully incorporated. The range of effects that can be achieved, along with the non-fraying qualities, highly commend this as a technique to consider using for a variety of projects.

Samples of boiling water and 'Solusheet' soluble fabrics.

Until recently, hand stitching has not been successful when worked on soluble cloth due to a number of reasons. In most cases, the stitches were not tight or dense enough to hold their structure in a unified manner when the fabric is washed away. Many of the thin 'plastic' type of film splits when thicker threads and large needles pierce the surface making the whole exercise very frustrating and not customer friendly. These inhibiting factors are now lessening due to two main innovations.

Firstly, both the 'organdy' type boiling water soluble cloth and the comparatively recent 'Solusheet' vilene from Japan react more like softer conventional materials when hand stitched with a good range of threads. There appears to be little or no splitting or tearing during the work process. Secondly, by planning and machining an under network of straight stitches, a wide range of hand stitches can be worked on, over, around and through the meshes to stabilise and link all the elements. With adequate experimentation, interesting hand stitched surfaces can be created exploiting the unique qualities of bolder textures within a lacy context thus offering the embroiderer a further choice of action to contemplate.

The most important technical factor to understand is that it is necessary to machine a network or mesh of straight stitches. This should be designed and worked before embarking on any hand stitches. The machine stitching not only provides the basic support structure but also the linking elements which prevents the work disintegrating or losing its shape when the background material is washed away.

Initially consider the quality of cloth you wish to create. A grid or mesh of single lines of straight stitches will give a softer more fragile effect even when supporting thick hand stitch threads. A network of straight stitches where two or three lines have been machined on top of each other will result in a stronger less flexible cloth.

Layers of straight stitches over stitched with zig-zag stitch will create a strong mesh and will allow the piece to hold its shape quite rigidly.

NB: Remember that a zig zag stitch worked on its own unravels when the fabric is washed away. It always needs to be worked over straight stitches for it to maintain its form.

Right:
A set of samples illustrating various meshes under pinning the surface stitches.

A) A machined mesh with solid areas allowing for easier fastening on and off procedures.

B) A similar mesh (as above) hand stitched in a toning thread using buttonhole stitch haphazardly placed and including little jet beads in the work process. Due to the single lines of machine stitch, this piece drapes softly.

C) This sample shows that the machined lines were overstitched with zig - zag stitch using a metallic thread which resulted in a rigid structure.

D) It was then embellished with French knots and beads.

E) A sketch showing the undermesh of machine stitches to support (f).

F) This geometric mesh is adorned with straight stitches and double layered cross stitches giving a chunky result.

G) A sketch showing the undermesh of machine stitches to support (h).

H) A simple arrangement of machined straight stitches with rows of buttonhole stitch worked in a range of fine threads. These were fastened on and off in the slightly heavier edge.

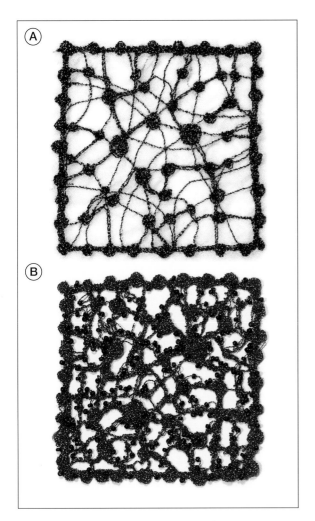

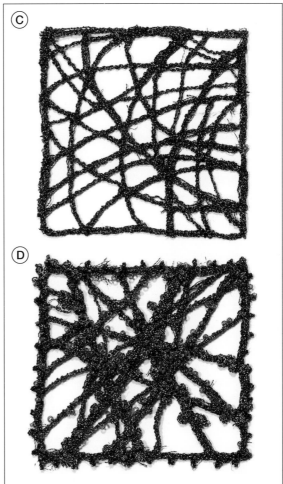

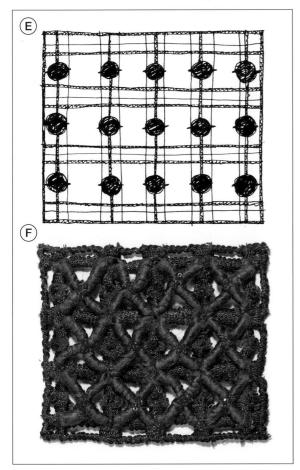

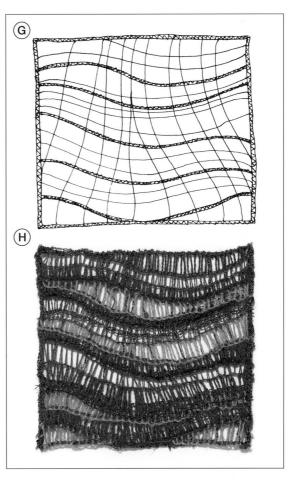

Previously threads manufactured for hand stitching had a limited use when considered alongside soluble fabrics. Snippets and off cuts of yarns can be arranged between two layers of soluble film as a 'sandwich' and machined in place linking them one to another to form a network resulting in an attractive lacy fabric when the ground cloth is washed away. Great care needs to be taken with the initial placement of the yarns and the rhythmic patterning of the machine stitches echoing the arrangement of the threads. As well as ensuring that all the elements are linked, the colour and tone of the machine thread needs to be carefully considered so that all the sections within the piece appear unified.

The linking mesh of straight stitches may emphasise the geometric or criss cross patterning, circular movements or simple flowing lines.

To avoid disappointment, work out the supporting structure of machine stitches before embarking on a project. Practice on trial sized machined meshes. This action is always worthwhile and allows you to make any mistakes as well as giving the opportunity of sorting any adjustments.

The 'organdy' type of fabric, pale blue in colour, which needs to be boiled has several advantages. As already stated, it looks and feels like a sheer fabric and therefore machine and hand stitching can be worked on it quite enjoyably. When the fabric is washed away, the quality of the resulting cloth is much softer. The disadvantages are the actual boiling process particularly within a classroom situation and hand dyed or fragile threads may loose some colour or spoil the textural finish.

Unless the embroidery is very large it is always advisable to carefully pin and stretch it on a piece of Styrofoam or polystyrene sheet to maintain its shape, structure and to limit any shrinkage when submerged in the boiling water. (see 'Vanishing Act' - book 1).

The comparatively new 'Solusheet' vilene made in Japan is a delightful fabric to work on and is made in two weights. The thicker one has certainly proved to be most successful with little evidence of tearing whether working many layers of machine stitches, fine filigree work or textural hand stitches. Stitching through it with a large size 14 chenille needle and a variety of yarns and tapes seems extremely workable. The fabric washes away in cold or warm water so making it more suitable to use in

a classroom as well as being less harsh to hand dyed and novelty threads. It may be cautionary to pin out a fragile structure before immersing it in water.

The heavier 'plastic' type of soluble film although extremely useful for making a range of machine laces, particularly the 'sandwich' method', may inhibit the energetic hand stitcher using chunkier threads. Very thin soluble stabilisers now on the market tear far too easily for intensive hand stitching. New materials appear in the shops at regular intervals so always be ready to try them.

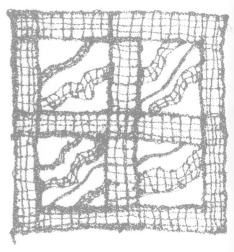

Above: A drawing of a proposed grid. It could be worked in a variety of ways. Canvas work stitches such as tent or velvet as well as chain or stem could be worked on it. Brooches and other motifs could be created knowing that the edges will not fray and the problem of neatening an edge of a conventional cloth is eliminated.

Left: Haphazardly placed rectangular grids of machine stitches decorated with stem stitch and chrystal beads.

Right: Diagram showing a grid arrangement and the proposed area of machined 'fabric' where the threads to be darned can be machined or hand sewn to secure in place.

Far Right: A darned grid using embroidery, knitting yarns and fabric strips.

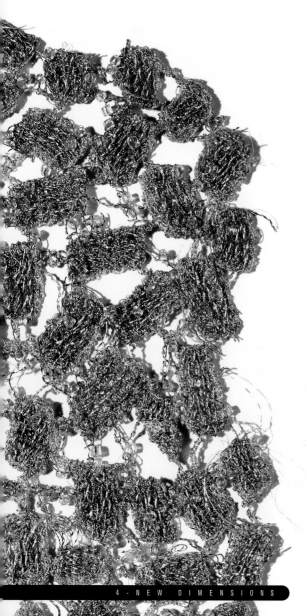

Making a Start

Machining a straight stitched grid is probably the easiest and most effective way to start and to understand the methodology of this particular approach of combining hand and machine stitching on soluble fabric.

Initially machine the grids following the lines drawn or traced through with a pencil. These could be arranged vertically, diagonally or with wavy lines. The spaces between need not be uniform. Some of the lines could be layered or 'zig zagged' to thicken or made up of single lines for a more lacy effect. The most important factor is to remember to strengthen or slightly overstitch edges so that the structure holds its shape when topped with hand stitches. ALWAYS CHECK THAT ALL LINES JOIN PARTICULARLY AT THE OUTER EDGES.

An effective use of a grid is to darn under and over the mesh with a variety of threads and / or torn strips of fabric. Wonderful colourful schemes where the tones and textures have been carefully considered can be developed into some innovative materials. This approach can result in some attractive fabrics suitable to front a waistcoat or vest or decorative additions to clothing and accessories such as bags or scarves.

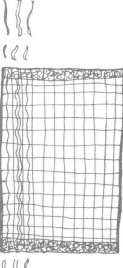

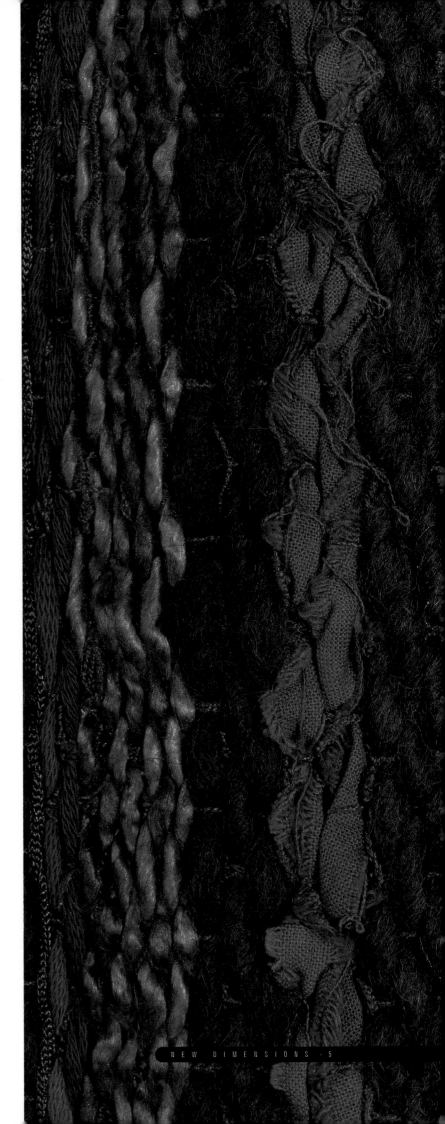

Fastening On & Off

After some experimentation with small trial samples you will find it easier to plan the outer edges of the work and the resolution to fastening on and off your hand stitch threads especially the thicker ones.

In some instances it may be desirable to create a new 'fabric' by machining a mesh or network of straight stitches on the soluble cloth on the outer edges or within certain areas of your proposed design.

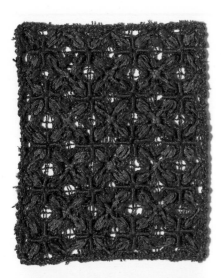

This procedure will make it easier to fasten the threads neatly with a double stitch. On completion of the hand stitches further machine stitching can be worked to hide and / or integrate the thread ends. An alternative method could be to fasten the threads with a knot on the soluble cloth a little away from the proposed stitching area. Many canvas workers use this method darning the end into the back of the stitches. If this is not appropriate due to the scale or lack of density of the hand stitches, a narrow machine stitched edge could be worked after the hand stitching has been completed so securing the ends as well as providing an attractive and strengthened border.

Ideally these actions should be determined when planning the design so it does not appear as a mismatched afterthought. As already mentioned trimming the knots away and darning the ends into the back of the work could be another solution as long as the stitching is bold enough to accommodate this action.

These three attractive samples have been worked by Gay Eaton from New Zealand. She is the author of 'Wessex Stitchery' and kindly accepted the challenge of machining a grid of straight stitches to work variations in this technique.

Above: *This sample shows 'Exeter' pattern including long tail fly and spiders web stitches in No.8 perle and stranded cottons.*

Left: *'Wanaka Maze' in No.8 perle and stranded cottons.Long tail chain, fly and short tailed chain are featured.*

Lower Left: *'Wanaka Maze' worked in a No.5 perle.*

Many counted thread techniques and canvas work stitches could be worked over machined meshes on soluble cloth with fascinating results.

Use of Surface Stitches

Any composite surface stitch can use the grid for support. They include raised stem band, raised chain band and lock stitch to mention a few. These can be decorated further by layering, wrapping or beading to achieve an encrusted surface.

Other knotted or chained stitches need a junction or crossed threads to enmesh them. Slight adjustments may have to be made so that each stitch holds its shape when the soluble fabric is washed away. Additional stitching to layer or decorate also helps their stability.

Fly, feather and various buttonhole stitches offer further lace works to consider. Overlapping them creates new patterns so extending the possibilities.

Single lines of machined stitching worked in diagonal and straight grid arrangements provided the base network for the following samples.

Above: *Double knot , stem and knotted cable chain have been worked in bold yarns and encrusted with beads.*

Right: *This grid is stem stitched incorporating beads .The solid bands are worked with sorbello stitch and beads. Both pieces hang beautifully and work well as a decorative cuffs.*

Couching can also be very effective. In order to anchor the stitch firmly, a machine stitched 'fabric' may need to be made in the first instance so that a secure base is set up before working the stitch into it. This only needs to be the width of the intended stitchery.

• Although much of the machine stitching will be covered always plan the colour carefully at the outset to unify the piece.

• All hand stitching, beading and securing thread ends should be completed before dissolving or washing away the soluble fabric.

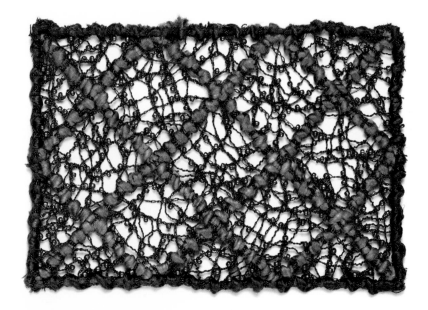

• Interesting, non-fraying decorative edges can be created.

• Fabric applied by tacking, basting or bonding offers another creative avenue to exploit. The fabric shapes contrast well with hand stitching and also provide a means behind which threads can be fastened on and off.

• Machining lines with the machine set for normal can also make simple grids and networks. This action can be tedious and time consuming but it does enable the dedicated hand stitcher to develop these surfaces without having a consuming passion or the ability for free motion machining.

• The weight of the hand stitches can effect the drape and hang of the new cloth. Interesting surfaces can be created.

Top:
A simple diagonal mesh (see right) was over stitched with Bokhara couching on the main lines and fine buttonhole stitch incorporating beads on the randomly stitched mesh.

Above:
The same sized network but stitched with bold wools in Romanian couching, partially wrapped and knotted. Single sorbello stitches are worked over the mesh.

Dissolving the Support Fabric

Creating a fabric to insert within a garment, to make a little bag, a decorative cuff, a brooch or to be an integral part of a panel or hanging all require a different tactile quality from soft draping to a hard edged fixed shape.

The dissolving process can also influence the drape, firmness or stiffness of the fabric. The stitched piece can be plunged into the appropriate water temperature depending on the fabric type in order to remove the soluble cloth. When it appears clear of the original material but feels slightly sticky to touch, a little of the fabric residue left within the stitches will result in a stiffish finish when dry. Further rinses will gradually clear the newly stitched fabric of all traces effecting the feel of the cloth depending on the build up or density of the machine or hand stitching. A final rinse in fabric conditioner may also help to achieve a finer, softer feel to the finished cloth.

To maintain the size and shape:

• It is helpful to pin out fragile structures on to polystyrene before immersing with water. These can be left in place to dry or carefully removed and re-stretched by pinning onto a corkboard.

• Having measured the size, larger pieces can be placed into a sink or bath of water to dissolve away the soluble cloth and rolled in a towel to remove excess water before pinning out to the original size on a piece of insulation or notice board (or similar).

Left:
A diagram showing under mesh of machined stitches which preceded the surface stitching shown below.

Below:
This simple interpretation of a colourful garden where over lapping cross stitches cover the central panel, stem stitches decorate the border and knotted cable chain and beads represent the flowers.

Further Ideas

A huge range of primary design sources can inspire assymmetrical or freer machined networks. Flower gardens, rocks, tree bark, water patterns could all suggest pleasing shapes, colour schemes and textural ideas to stylise, simplify or exaggerate. Contrasting bolder vibrant hand stitches with delicate machine stitched tracery or stitching finer hand stitches on a machined mesh to produce a fragile cloth may well extend your stitch dictionary and suggest new challenges.

• As with most stitched pieces whatever the method, care should be taken to design any patterns within the given shape and as appropriate to the function of the artefact.

• Contrast busy areas with quieter or more restrained ones.

• Consider the positioning or effect of dimensional or flat surfaces.

• Select textural or colourful highlights, focal points or other visual devices to add emphasis or lift the piece from being too bland. This would be appropriate for an item but not if the stitching was a supporting section within part of a larger concept.

• Remember to consider reflecting a colour or texture throughout the work for unity.

As previously mentioned, this is a comparatively new method of working which was introduced in 'Stitch Magic'. It is an exciting technique which has great potential. It is hoped that many embroiderers will take up the challenge and create original stitched textiles exploiting their own style and interests.

Right:
Sketches showing the simple arrangements of small fabric pieces and linking machine stitches which preceded the hand stitched sample (right).

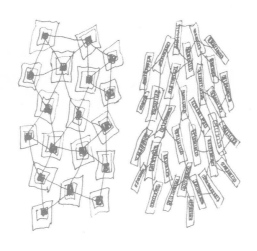

Left: *This interpretation shows an abstracted view looking through leaves. Scraps of synthetic fabric were linked by single lines of machining with double layers of single sorbello stitch topped with a bead worked on each piece of fabric. The weight of the wool stitches effected the hang of the cloth.*

Red and pink fabric were overstitched with blocks of straight stitches in a variety of threads.

Far Left: *Stem, straight stitches and beads worked in wools, silks and cottons. This was a trial sample inspired by seaweed and stones on a tide line.*

A

B

This page:
Experimental samples showing:
A) Blocks of straight stitches worked
in silk thread on fragments of fabric
connected by single lines of machine
stitching.
B) As above with the addition of
knotted cable chain worked in
purple wool.

This Page:
*Hand stitching on black cotton velvet
with machine stitching over.
(detail approx. 40cms x 20cms).*

Hand Stitching for Machine Embroidery - by Jean

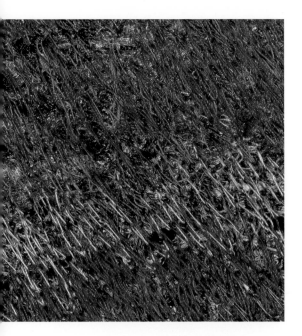

Mention the words 'hand stitching' to many confirmed machine embroiderers and they will blanch at the thought. Contemporary machines are capable of so many functions that it is rarely necessary to use a hand held needle and thread. Hopefully in the next few pages even the most ardent machine embroidery fan will want to pick up a needle and thread as a means of adding a rich and textured surface to their vocabulary.

There are many advantages of working in this way not the least being that it can work up very fast with the use of bold threads and large stitches.

Some people have said that there is little point in hand stitching if it is going to be covered afterwards but that is to miss the whole idea. The hand stitching is echoed and enriched, not totally swamped and this depends on the sensitivity of the machine stitching. Heavy hand stitching that has been further machined can offer a very robust surface useful in decorative domestic contexts.

On large-scale wall or practical pieces the working of a base of dimensional hand stitching offers a refreshing change of scale in contrast to the finer machine line. It is therefore a useful tool when altering the quality of the mark.

Starting
An hour or two practising on structured samples will help achieve sensitivity to the basic elements of this technique. The sampler illustrated (opposite) shows a series of four textures that exploit a range of hand-stitch marks that have proved very useful for larger pieces of work.

Guidelines for Hand stitching.
• Begin with a limited colour range so as to focus on the texture and technique.

• Use thick bold threads as fine threads could become swamped.

• Select a strong neutral open weave fabric such as heavy cotton for ease of hand stitching.

• The needle is important, particularly when using thick threads. Many are put off because it is tough to pull the thread through the fabric and subsequently avoid doing it. The use of a large chenille needle such as a 14 will ease the path of the thread.

• Tack or mark small rectangles (5cms x 3.5cms or 2" x 11/2") as guidelines.

• Select the appropriate stitches and work them.

The following four exercises offer a range of effects which students have found particularly useful and are the basis of the staged sampler (opposite).

a) Simple linear straight stitches
b) knotted cable chain and French knots
c) a regular grid combining lines and knots
d) irregular straight stitches worked in a simple flowing movement.

These textures cover the basic elements for the success of this technique.

Machine Stitch Guidelines
Set the machine for free motion embroidery

• Select a good tempered thread that tones with the hand stitching and remember that the intensity of the machine mark causes it to look darker so a fraction lighter might work even better.

• Shaded threads can work well but be aware that those with a wide colour and tonal range may offer colour irregularities that can overwhelm the balance.

• Frame the work as tautly as possible in a tambour frame with a bound inner ring.

• For this technique it is particularly helpful to use a darning foot to hold the ground firmly and prevent thread breakage.

• It is a good idea to begin with the straight stitches and start SLOWLY. The idea is to echo the hand stitching working back and forth filling the spaces between the stitches nibbling into the edge of the threads to secure but not flatten them. In a short time the contrast between the raised bold stitches and the flatter machine textures will be evident.

Left:
Tree texture sample. Multicoloured machine stitching over hand stitch.

• Progress onto the knotted texture and again start very slowly. Before beginning it is a good idea to think out a pathway so that you may keep up a rhythm. Many people think that the machine carries them away but the point of these exercises is to show that we can have control and the hand stitching offers a structure to focus on. I find the top left corner is the best and then work swinging movements that echo the circular shapes edging gently into the knots to 'marry' them into the ground. Do not stitch into the thick of a large knot as it may break the needle. Any gaps can be filled in sensitively at the end.

• The third sample shown provides an opportunity for a combination of straight and circular movements.

• There are times when this technique is useful in a part rather than to cover the whole ground. (see page 23) so this simple exercise will offer the opportunity to practise blending into the background.

Armed with these simple strategies a huge array of textural possibilities opens up. Each element can be exploited in numerous ways so try varying the colours and stitches. These samples illustrate straight machine stitching only so the huge range available on most modern machines including zigzag and pre set stitch patterns offer an astonishing palette for textured surfaces.

Right:
Hand and machine stitch sampler - see text.

Other Stitches

The simple stitches previously
described work well but the hand
stitch vocabulary is limitless and
use of other appropriate stitches
will depend on subject matter.

Once sensitivity to machining
over a pre stitched ground has
been achieved then select stitches
that describe different surfaces.

Before starting, work out the
function of the hand stitching
within the context of the design.
Is it to be line, texture, pattern
or organic rhythms?

Architectural details might
require a decorative treatment
and detached chain or 'lazy
daisy' might prove effective.

In the piece illustrated (above)
detached chain has been used to
indicate the patterning and the
arch with machine stitching
worked sympathetically in a
toning thread. Any stitch may be
used in this way.

Exploiting Colour

Never underestimate the power of one colour on itself. It can provide great richness and expose the raised structures through cast shadows.

White or cream textures are very satisfying and in the cushion illustrated thick silk threads have been contrasted with matt machine threads to give a subtle overall pattern. Black on black would work equally well.

The resulting cloth can be robust, hard wearing and very useful in accessories such as bags, waistcoats, belts or other domestic applications.

When approaching embroidery on wearables consider the fabric as a whole cloth, rather than decorating parts of the item. This combined with the subtle richness of one colour on itself could result in sophisticated finished pieces.

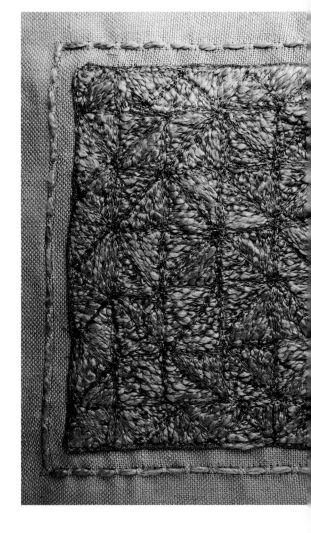

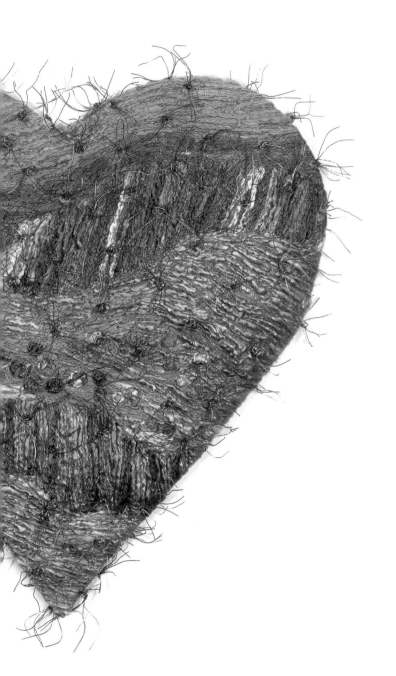

Multi-colours
Simple and effective undulating surfaces may be achieved with machine stitching by echoing the tones and colours of the hand stitching.
This allows the focus to be concentrated on the undulations of the surface.

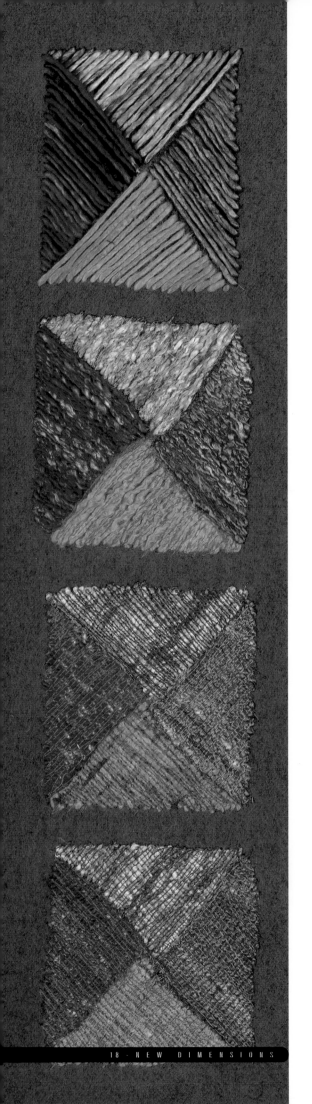

Colour Counter Rhythms

Having established a range of machine textures that echo hand stitching then further dramatic effects are possible by colour mixing and over stitching.

So far we have looked at harmonious and co-ordinated textures. Instead of using a tonal machine thread then use a contrasting thread for visual impact. It is often wise to us the contrast in the same tonal range such as dark orange with dark blue, but there are always exceptions that prove the rule.

Using different colours as ground fabrics will also alter the look of the stitching even if the background is completely covered. Consider the way painters often use a colour under-painting their compositions to give a feel of warmth or evoke an atmosphere.

The exercises on this page (left) were worked on a blue acrylic felt that was easy to stitch into.

(A)

• The same pattern and colours of straight stitches underpinned each sample.

• Tonal threads matching the colour were worked into the first layer of stitching much as in the very first sample.

• Each colour was moved round one section and stitched at right angles to the first stitches for a colour blended effect

• The same thing was repeated and so on.

Machine tensions vary but when working over several layers of stitching you may find it easier to loosen the top tension.

The resulting cloth is thick and rich and although the initial stitches are only faintly visible the resulting surface has a rich complexity that could prove useful for the future.

The staged samples illustrated (below) show the various stages carried out when completing textured stitching on heavy black cotton velvet).

A) The colour was discharged and printed (see 'Voluptuous Velvet' - book 2) in a simple counter-changed diagonal pattern.

B) Strong silk straight stitches added further texture to the ground.

C) Several layers of machine stitching were worked using varying colours and angles to achieve a rich but simple texture.

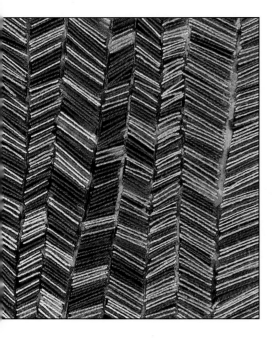

C

Background Fabrics

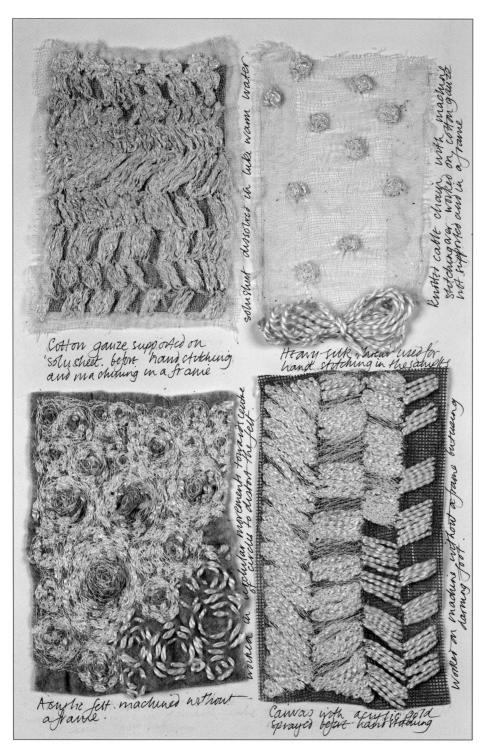

Handwritten notes on the notebook page:

Cotton gauze supported on 'solusheet' before hand stitching and machining in a frame

solusheet dissolved in luke warm water

Knotted cable chain stitching worked on cotton gauze not supported and in a frame

Heavy silk thread used for hand stitching in the squares

worked in a circular movement towards centre of circle to distort the felt.

Acrylic felt machined without a frame.

worked on machine without a frame but using darning foot.

Canvas with acrylic gold sprayed before hand stitching

Above: *Notebook page (see text).*

Starting with a firm fabric helps to build up confidence in this simple but effective technique. Other fabrics will offer different possibilities and time spent looking at a range of backgrounds will show just how versatile this method of texturing a cloth can be.

Thick fabrics work easily and well but finer fabrics can be successfully incorporated providing some simple guidelines are followed.

• For gauzes, scrims and other fine fabrics it helps to apply them to a water-soluble fabric such as 'Solusheet' to support them. for hand and machine stitching.

• By holding the two fabrics firmly in a frame it is possible to work bold stitches.

• It should be remembered that when the soluble fabric is 'melted' away the threads on the reverse will be exposed so it is necessary to be tidy with finishing off and not make large jumps from stitch to stitch if this will interfere with the final look.

• After working the hand stitch then proceed with the machine stitching as desired and when complete cut away the excess soluble fabric.

• Finally immerse the fabric in cold water to remove the backing (see 'Vanishing Act' - book 1) and pin it out on board or polystyrene to stretch the final piece. For fragile pieces pin them to polystyrene before adding water to help the fabric keep its shape whilst dissolving the support.

It is particularly satisfying to see the contrast between the chunky textured stitches and the fine ground fabric.

On the other end of the scale thick piled velvets and textured fabrics can look most effective. Knitting of various sorts is often neglected because of its strong characteristic pattern but contrast it with machine stitching and an exotic and robust fabric could emerge.
It is a wonderful way of recycling favourite knitted garments.
The two samples (below) on this page show a colourful knitted piece that has been cut and applied to a firm background to support it before being hand stitched with bold colours, using fly stitch to echo the rhythms.
It already has a very vibrant pattern so the aim is to add richness and contrast.
After the hand stitching a neutral machine thread was used to echo the fly stitches and flatten the pile in areas to give different levels. This could be wonderful for cushions, throws, bags and accessories or sections of wall hangings.

The notebook page illustrated (left) here shows samples worked on contrasting fabrics. Gauze, canvas and felt offer a range of surfaces and effects.

The samples were worked in white on white for comparisons but monochrome work can be dyed after completion providing the fibres are compatible with the dyes. It is easy to mistake a polyester for a cotton thread and this will affect the way the dye is accepted.

For most fine to medium quality fabrics it is advisable to keep the fabric taut in a frame.
Alternatively if the background is sufficiently firm then holding it taut with both hands whilst machining will work well.
But there are times when it is a positive advantage to allow the fabric to distort when working. Felt is excellent for this purpose as it is firm but flexible and there are excellent wool viscose or acrylic felts that handle well.

Work the hand stitching as previously described in or out of a frame according to preference and then place it under the darning foot before holding it firmly with both hands.
The fabric will distort and is excellent for organic effects.

Above:
Machine set for free motion embroidery using a darning foot and no foot (see text).

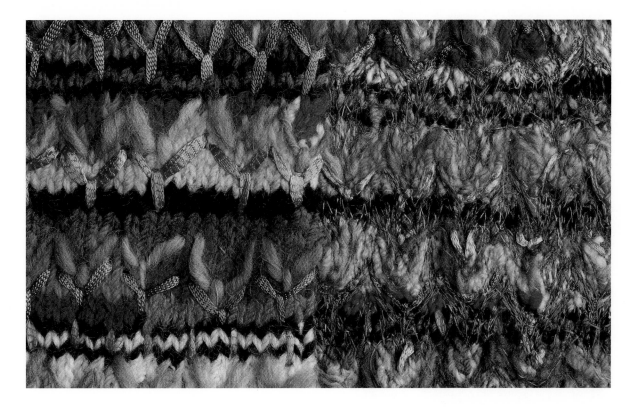

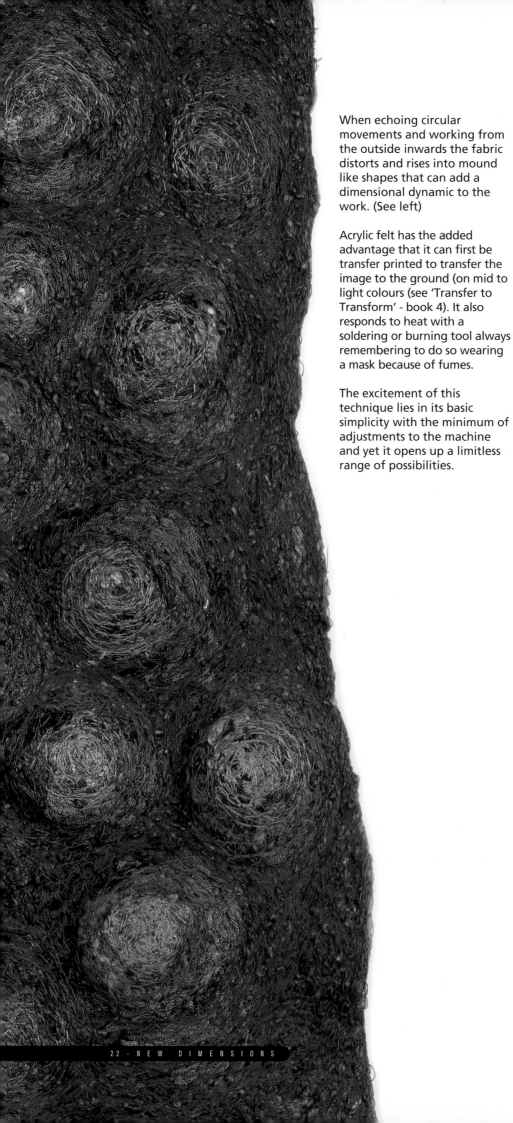

When echoing circular movements and working from the outside inwards the fabric distorts and rises into mound like shapes that can add a dimensional dynamic to the work. (See left)

Acrylic felt has the added advantage that it can first be transfer printed to transfer the image to the ground (on mid to light colours (see 'Transfer to Transform' - book 4). It also responds to heat with a soldering or burning tool always remembering to do so wearing a mask because of fumes.

The excitement of this technique lies in its basic simplicity with the minimum of adjustments to the machine and yet it opens up a limitless range of possibilities.

Used as an overall texture or part of a mixed media piece it can provide a vigorous change of scale.

It can be used to blend heavily textured areas into backgrounds by controlled gradations of hand and machine stitching.

When using robust threads the resulting fabric is tremendously hard wearing and practical.

Multi-layered and dimensional cloths may be achieved by the rhythmic working of carefully coloured machine stitching onto prepared grounds.

On reading through it is hoped that even the most fanatical machine stitcher might be tempted to add to their vocabulary with some of these possibilities.

We have only scratched on the surface of the potential and look forward to continuing and developing this area.

Having worked some of the suggested samples you will be able to incorporate the aspects of these techniques that appeal and make them your own.

All the samples could be turned into simple cards or small items but for future reference we suggest keeping them as a reference bank as part of an ongoing exploration of the excitement of machine and hand stitched textiles.

Left: *See text.*

Right:
*'Tree Texture' (30cms x 20cms).
Mixed media paper and fibre
layers with hand and machine
stitch additions.*

Stockists

Gillsew
Boundary House,
Moor Common,
Lane End, High Wycombe,
Bucks. HP14 3HR
Tel: 01494 881886
(general supplies, threads)

Husqvarna Studio
90, Lower Parliament St
Nottingham. NG1 1EH
Tel. 0115 988 1550
(Vilene Solusheet -
water soluble fabric)

Art Van Go
The Studios, 1 Stevenage Rd.,
Knebworth, Herts. SG3 6AN
Tel. 01438 814946
(general supplies, Fron Isaf
threads)

Oliver Twists
22 Phoenix Rd.,
Crowther, Washington,
Tyne and Wear. NE38 OAD
Tel. 0191 4166016
(hand and machine threads)

Mulberry Silks
Patricia Wood
Silkwood,
4 Park Close, Tetbury,
Glos. GL8 8HS
Tel: 01666 503438
(silk hand threads)

Variegations
Rose Cottage,
Harper Royd Lane,
Halifax. HX6 3QQ
Tel. 01422 832411
(assorted materials, threads)

Barnyarns
Brickyard Rd.,
Boroughbridge,
York. YO51 9NS
Tel. 0870 8708586
(general supplies, machine threads)

Inca Studio
10 Duke St.,
Princes Risborough,
Bucks. HP27 OAT
Tel: 01844 343343
(general supplies, threads)

Texere Threads
College Mill,
Barkerend Road,
Bradford. BD1 4AU
Tel: 0871 7171129

Whaleys (Bradford) Ltd.
Harris Court
Bradford. BD7 4EQ
Tel: 01274 576718
(background fabrics)

Suggested Reading

The Art of the Needle
Jan Beaney - Century

A Complete Guide to Creative
Embroidery
Jan Beaney, Jean Littlejohn.
Batsford Books.

Stitch Magic
Jan Beaney, Jean Littlejohn.
Batsford Books

Machine Embroidery Stitch
Techniques
Valery Campbell-Harding and
Pamela Watts. Batsford Books.

Double Trouble

Booklets in this series include:

1 - Vanishing Act
2 - Voluptuous Velvet
3 - Bonding & Beyond
4 - Transfer to Transform
5 - Gardens & More
6 - Conversations with Constance
7 - Trees as a Theme
8 - Giving Pleasure
9 - New Dimensions -
     in Hand & Machine Embroidery
10 - Double Vision -
      Personal Approaches to Work

Acknowledgements

For this book we would like to
thank Pfaff & Husqvarna Viking
for their generous support
throughout.
Photography - Michael Wicks
Book Production - Jason Horsburgh
All illustrations by authors unless
otherwise indicated.

Inside Back Cover:
'One rotten apple can...'
(detail 40cms x 30cms).
*The apples were worked in straight
stitches using heavy silk and rayon
threads on a linen ground. The first
layer of machine stitching enriched
the apples. The whole piece was then
applied to wadding before
machining the ground to throw the
apples into relief.*